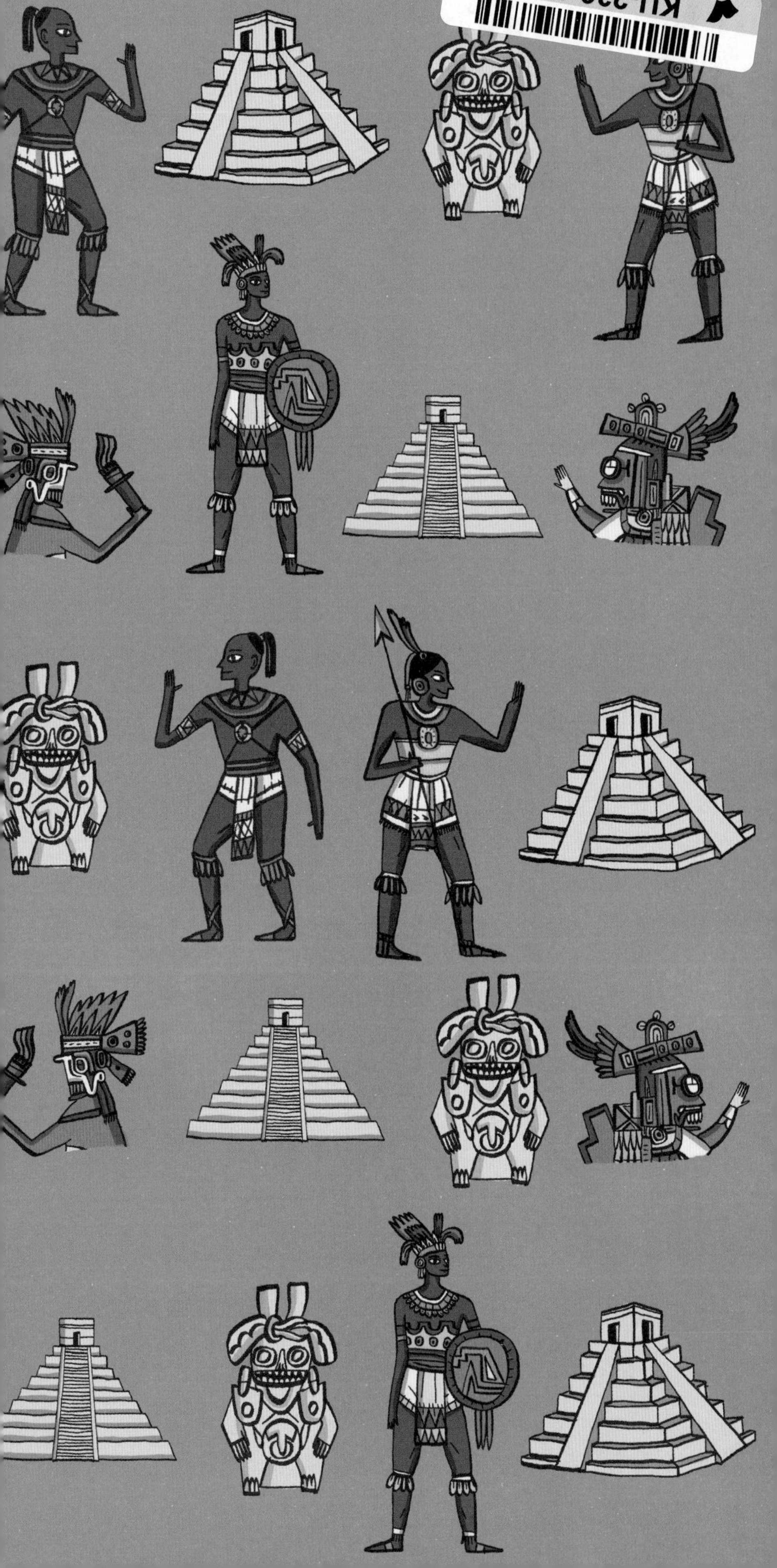

DISCOVER...

THE AZTEC EMPIRE

Illustrated by
Isabel Greenberg

Written by
Imogen Greenberg

Frances Lincoln
Children's Books

Welcome to the Aztec Empire

The Aztec Empire lasted for hundreds of years. The great emperors built vast cities and elaborate pyramid temples, waged war on their neighbors, and sacrificed their enemies to the gods. But who were the Aztecs really?

The Aztec Empire began as an alliance of three cities in Mesoamerica—a region of Central America. Through wars, trade, and treaties, they became more and more powerful. The emperor ruled the empire from the great city of Tenochtitlán, which is now Mexico City, and was a vast complex built across a great lake.

The Aztecs are known for their elaborate architecture and fearsome warriors. Even though they were pretty amazing, you'll find out in this book that the Aztecs were normal people, just like us.

Today we know a lot about how they lived, thanks to historians and archaeologists. Historians spend their time reading the documents that the Aztecs left behind. Archaeologists dig up amazing Aztec ruins—from vast temples to local villages—so we know more about how these ancient people lived.

In this book, you will discover all kinds of secrets about the Aztecs...and if you're wondering where and when these things happened, turn to the back, where you'll find a fold-out map and timeline. Now, come and meet your guide!

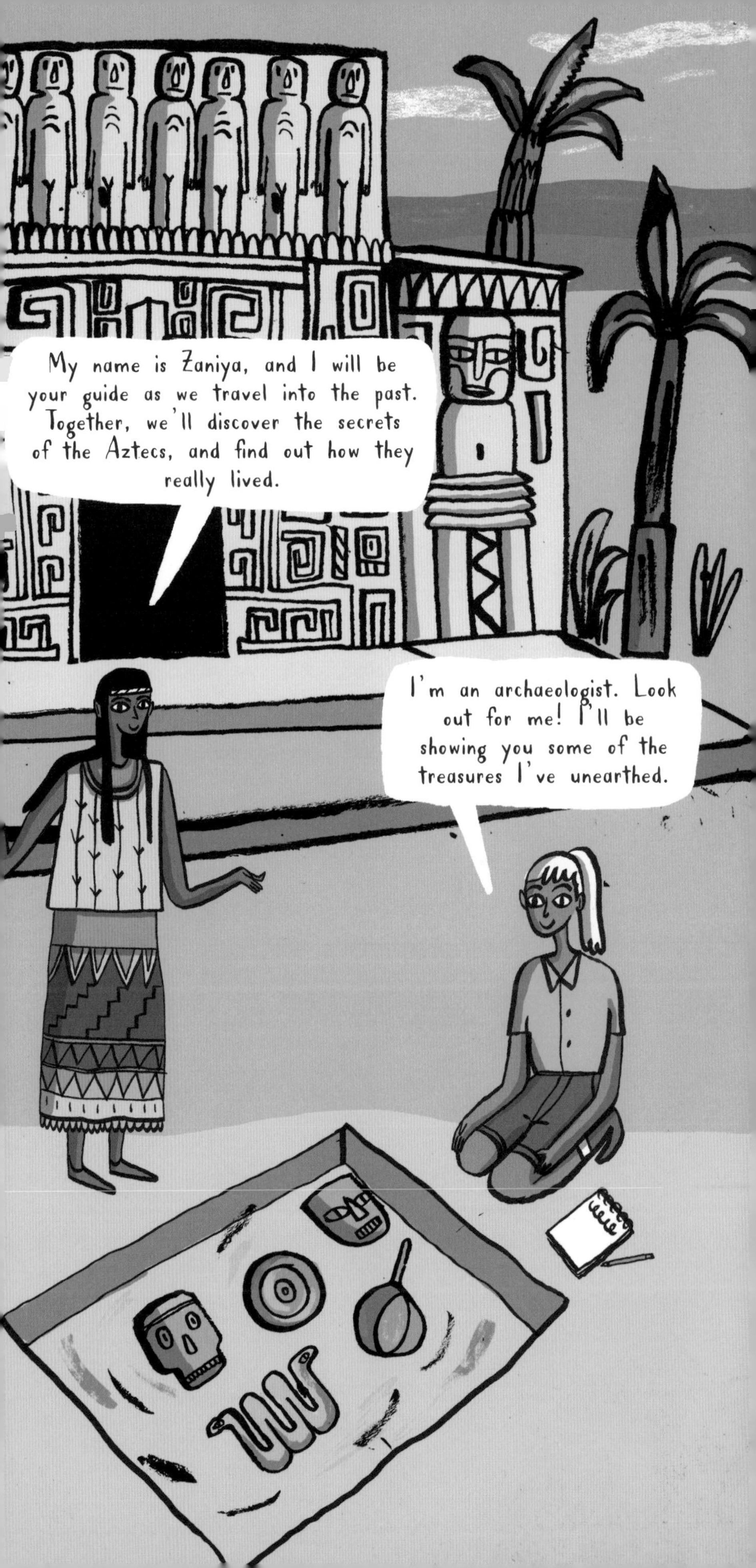
My name is Zaniya, and I will be your guide as we travel into the past. Together, we'll discover the secrets of the Aztecs, and find out how they really lived.
I'm an archaeologist. Look out for me! I'll be showing you some of the treasures I've unearthed.

The Aztec people lived in the plains of Mexico, where they fought fiercely against their neighbors to keep the empire strong. But the story goes that many years before they were a powerful empire, the Aztecs came from a place called Aztlán. Myths suggest that the god Huitzilopochtli had appeared before the people of Aztlán in a vision, and told them to set out on a journey to seek a new homeland.

Huitzilopochtli gifted them a bow and arrow. They set off on their sacred quest and journeyed for centuries to find their new homeland.

Eventually, around AD 1345, they reached an island in Lake Texcoco, where a priest had a vision.

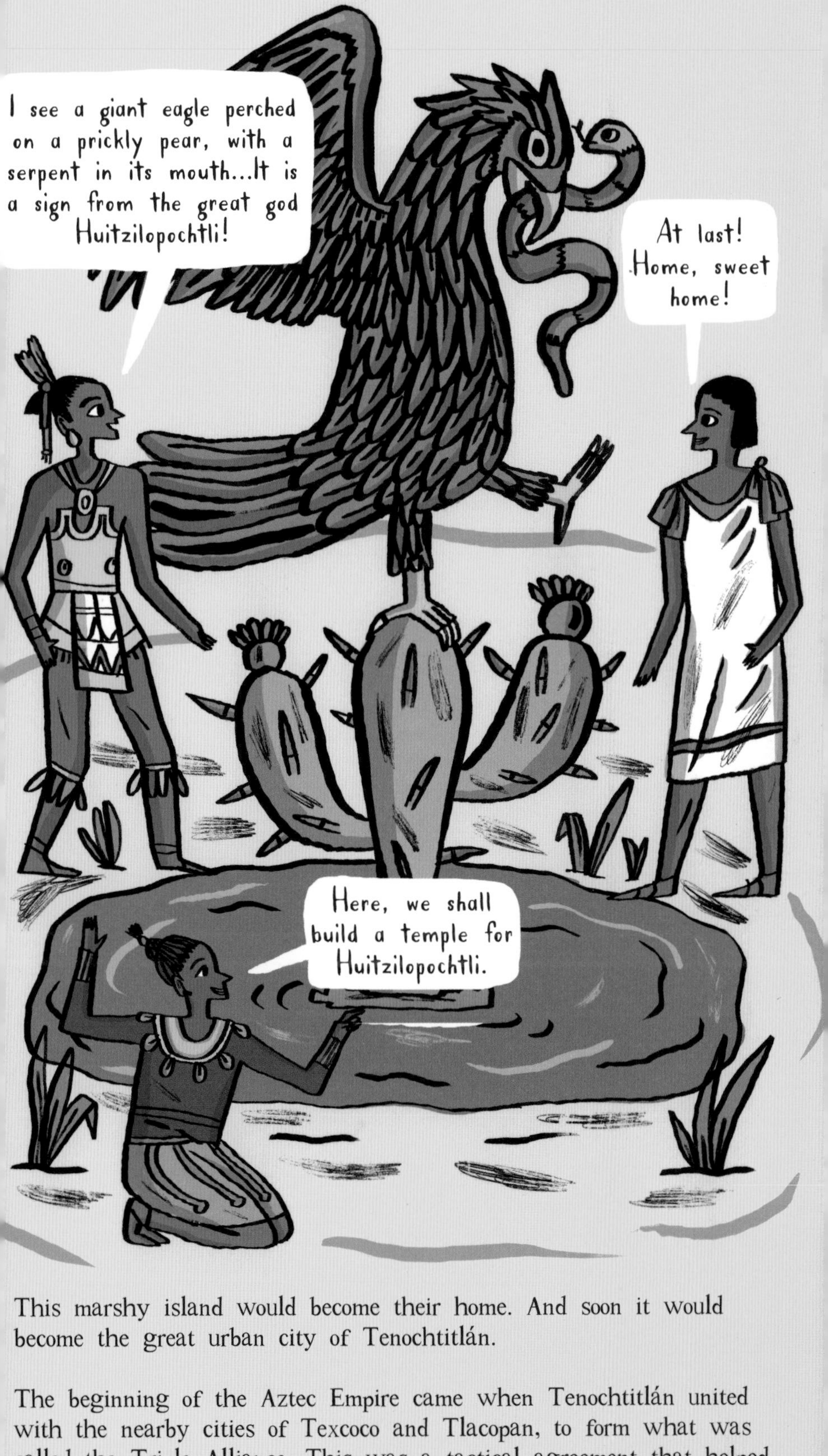
I see a giant eagle perched on a prickly pear, with a serpent in its mouth...It is a sign from the great god Huitzilopochtli!
At last! Home, sweet home!
Here, we shall build a temple for Huitzilopochtli.

This marshy island would become their home. And soon it would become the great urban city of Tenochtitlán.

The beginning of the Aztec Empire came when Tenochtitlán united with the nearby cities of Texcoco and Tlacopan, to form what was called the Triple Alliance. This was a tactical agreement that helped them to gather tributes (sort of like today's taxes) from the people, conquer more land, and expand the Aztec Empire.

HALL O

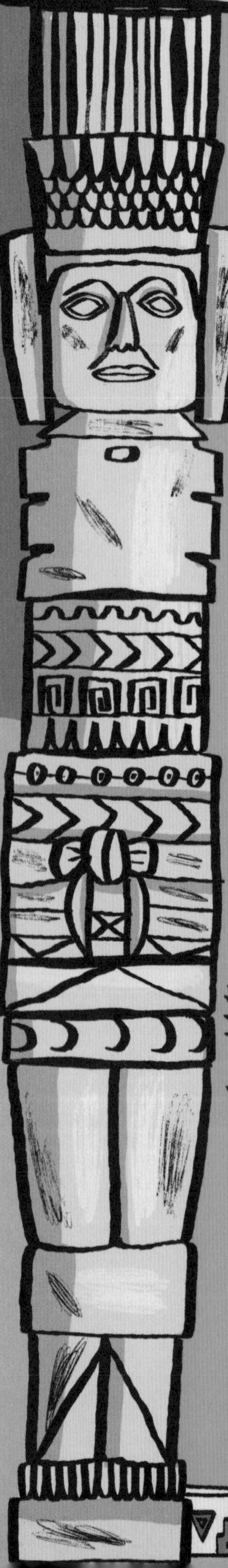

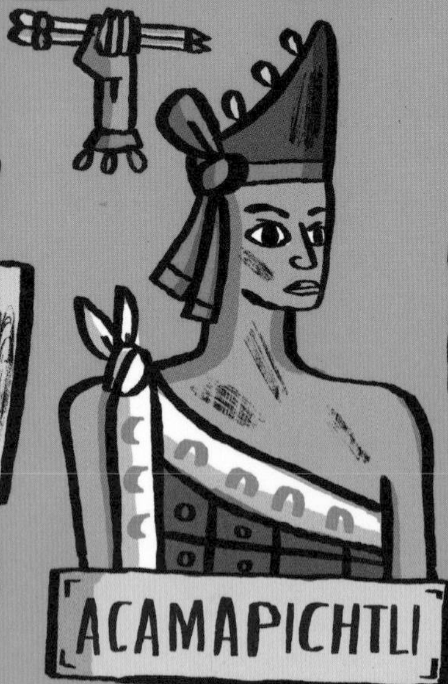
ACAMAPICHTLI

1376-1395
ACAMAPICHTLI was the first tlatoani (ruler) of the Aztecs o Tenochtitlán. He had 2 wives. After his death he was remembered as great warrior chief wh helped make the Aztecs strong.

1396-1417
HUITZILIHUITL was Acamapichtli's son. He was so fierce that he doubled his father's war conquests.

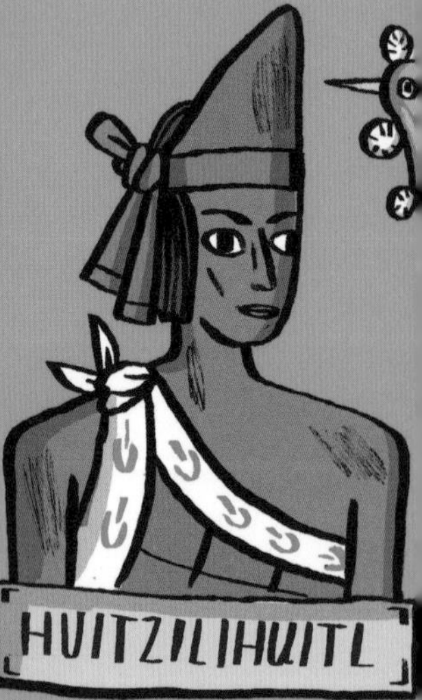
HUITZILIHUITL

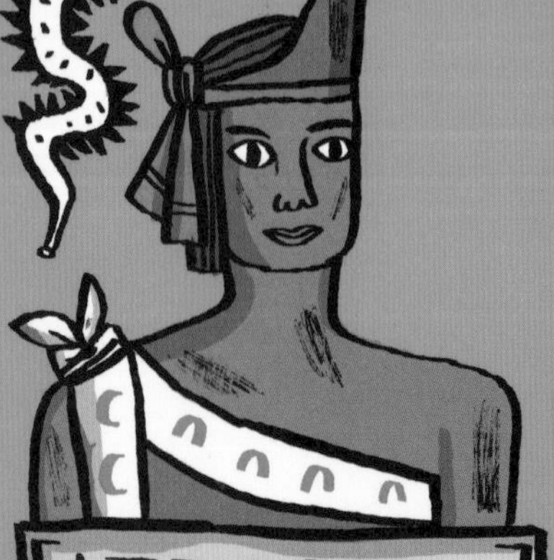
ITZCOATL

1427-1440
ITZCOATL united the rulers of the cities of Tenochtitlán, Tlacopan, and Texcoco into the Triple Alliance, which was the foundation of the Aztec Empire.

FAME

1440-1469
MOCTEZUMA ILHUICAMINA was a great military warrior. He was known to be serious, severe, and virtuous.

MOCTEZUMA ILHUICAMINA

1481-1486
TIZOC was not a very strong ruler. There are even rumors that he was poisoned by his own royal household—though others say he fell ill.

TIZOC

1502-1520
MOCTEZUMA II was a successful military leader, and the Aztec Empire was at its largest under his rule. He lived lavishly and may have had up to 200 wives.

MOCTEZUMA II

Tenochtitlán was one of the largest cities in the world at the time, with over 200,000 inhabitants. As the island city was built on water, it was carefully irrigated. It had huge green spaces and lush gardens abundant with animals and crops.

From the center of the city, nine causeways spread out to other linked settlements. Through canals and causeways, people and goods came to the city from all over the empire, and aqueducts brought fresh water to the people.

In the city center was a great imperial marKetplace, divided into sections where different things were sold.

On a feast day, it's estimated that up to 40,000 people could be trading here!

Three bags of corn, one bag of cocoa beans, and three chili peppers.

Coming right u

The Aztecs were incredible builders, and they were also extremely religious. In the middle of the city of Tenochtitlán was the Great Temple, built in the shape of a pyramid. It was part of a complex of around 80 religious buildings. Each Aztec leader added to the splendor of the temple as a gift to the gods.

Right, I've designed another pyramid. You know the drill!

Er, yes...er, remind me what a pyramid looks like again?

Call yourself an Aztec?! Bring me a new builder!

I want a new section added on the side. And I want it to say very clearly "For Huitzilopochtli, from Moctezuma Ilhuicamina."

Surely he knows that. He's a god, isn't he?

AZTEC CALENDAR

Aztec religion was centered on two important calendars. The first calendar was 260 days long and was called tonalpohualli, or the "day-count." It was used to divide the days between the gods, so religious ceremonies and rituals were spread evenly between them. It was important to keep the opposing forces of the gods in balance.

The days were divided fairly between all the gods who had to be worshipped equally, or they'd get very angry!

It's my celebration today!

I think you'll find it's mine! Check the calendar!

The second calendar was connected to agricultural practices and was 360 days long.

It was called xiuhpohualli, or the "year-count."

Every 52 years, the two calendars aligned and a cycle was completed. The Aztecs saw this as a time of enormous uncertainty, so to appease the gods they held the New Fire Ceremony—a festival lasting 12 days. At the beginning of the festival, all the fires in the city were extinguished. On the twelfth day, a sacrifice was made and a new fire was lit, signaling the beginning of the next 52-year cycle.

Religion played a very important role in daily Aztec life. They believed that gods, humans, and nature were all interconnected. For the Aztecs, the balance of nature depended on their worship of many different gods.

Meet the two most important Aztec gods!

Huitzilopochtli was the sun god, and also the god of war. Worship of Huitzilopochtli focused on keeping the sun alive.

Tlaloc was the rain god.

Sun, rain, and war were very important to people's lives. Peace meant prosperity, and good weather meant good crops.

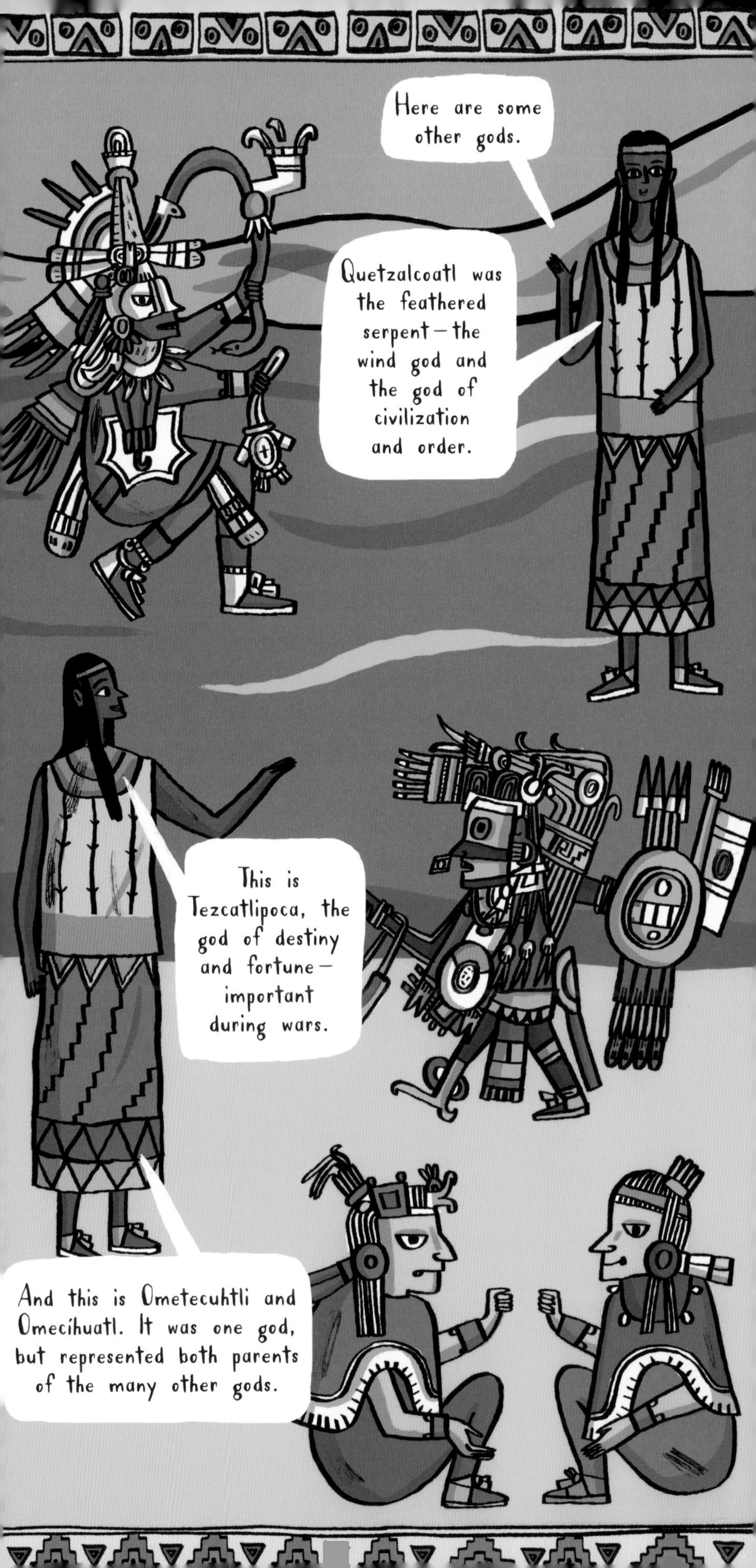
Here are some other gods.
Quetzalcoatl was the feathered serpent—the wind god and the god of civilization and order.
This is Tezcatlipoca, the god of destiny and fortune—important during wars.
And this is Ometecuhtli and Omecíhuatl. It was one god, but represented both parents of the many other gods.

LEGEND OF THE FIFTH SUN

The Aztecs believed the world was created and destroyed four times, and each world had a new sun. We are living in the age of the fifth sun. In the beginning, Ometecuhtli-Omecíhuatl created itself. As one being, it was good and bad, male and female, and chaos and order.

It had four children: Huitzilopochtli, Quetzalcoatl, Tezcatlipoca, and Xipe Totec. These four gods created the first world, but they also created the sea monster Cipactli, which began to devour everything. So the gods defeated it and created the universe from the monster.

To complete the world, there had to be a sun. But suns could only come into being through sacrifice. Tezcatlipoca sacrificed himself to become the first sun. But Quetzalcoatl and Tezcatlipoca fought, so Tezcatlipoca was knocked from the sky, destroying the world.

The gods fought with each other every time one of them sacrificed themselves to create a new sun. The world was destroyed four times until, eventually, our current world came into being. Nanahuatzin was the god who sacrificed himself this time, by jumping into a fire. Another god, Tecciztecatl, jumped after him. Nanahuatzin became a sun, and Tecciztecatl became a moon.

When Nanahuatzin's sun appeared in the sky, it paused and began to wobble. The other gods had to sacrifice their blood, too, so that the sun could rise up in the sky. Then the cycle of our sun and moon began.

HUMAN SACRIFICE

Humans imitated the sacrifices of the gods through sacrifices of their own, believing they appeased the gods and kept the sun alive. Religious festivals were great ceremonial events where sacrifices were made. There were offerings of meat, fruits, wine, and ceremonial objects, all of which were important to the gods.

Blood was even more precious. Sometimes worshippers would shed their own blood or that of an animal. But the most extreme sacrifice of all was to sacrifice another human being...They were often captured warriors or slaves.

AFTERLIFE

The Aztecs believed that the way a person died determined where they spent their afterlife. Warriors who died in battle, people who sacrificed themselves, and women who died in childbirth were all taken to one of 13 Aztec heavens by the rays of the sun.

However, those who died of natural causes would go to Mictlan, the underworld. There, the dead had to pass through nine levels and many difficult challenges to get to their final resting place.

Warriors had a special place in Aztec society—because they were so often at war. The most elite and prestigious Aztec warriors were the Eagles and the Jaguars.

You could tell them apart by their clothes: Eagles had feathers on their headdresses, and Jaguars wore pelts on their backs. The higher you ranked, the more elaborate your dress became.

This guy looks pretty senior. Check out how many feathers he has!

The Eagles and Jaguars were usually from wealthy families. But people from other parts of society could work their way up in the army, too. Capturing prisoners was an important way to rise in status as a warrior. You were not a true Aztec warrior until you had captured your first prisoner.

Warriors carried a decorated shield. They fought with bows, spears, and the maquahuitl, which was a combination of a sword and a club.

CLASSES

Society was made up of classes. The macehualtin worked in service to the nobles, the pipiltin. They helped build public buildings, created goods to sell, and grew crops.

Hurry up with that digging. You've got tributes to pay!

Nobles didn't have to pay tributes (a type of tax) and were trained to become judges, administrators, and philosophers, and continue to rule.

The class with the least opportunities and freedom were the tlatlacotin—the slave class. They were forced into servitude usually for failing to pay debts or breaking the law. But they could work their way out of slavery. Those who didn't would remain in slavery and could be sold, or sacrificed to the gods.

What shall I do with you now?

If I work hard enough, I might be able avoid that sacrifice business.

CLOTHES

The Aztecs made their clothes from ayate fiber, which came from the maguey cactus. The cloth was dyed using natural substances that were traded around the empire.

Men wore loincloths and a tilmàtli, which was a type of cloak.

Women wore skirts and a blouse, or short-sleeved shirt. Nice, huh?

FOOD

The Aztecs were skilled in agriculture. They were able to grow crops using terraces and chinampas, which were artificial islands in the lake beds. Maize was the most important crop. It was ground into flour and could be made into breads. They also grew and ate beans, squash, chili peppers, tomatoes, potatoes, and chocolate, which was made from cocoa beans. The word chocolate comes from the Aztec word "chocolatl."

Well, this is delicious!

It's only chocolatl...

Something tells me this is going to be a hit worldwide!

Nah, don't be silly.

ART

One of the most famous Aztec craft skills was featherwork. Artisans weaved brightly-colored feathers from birds together to make beautiful cloaks and headdresses.

They were special and very expensive, and only the nobility were allowed to wear them.

Jewelry was made from expensive materials like gold, silver, copper, and jade, and was worn by the rich. The emperor would have had the most amazing necklaces and earrings of all, and everyone would have worn their favorite pieces out for special occasions.

That's some nice bling you have there. But not as good as mine, obviously.

Um, thanks.

POETRY

The highest form of art in Aztec culture was poetry. Poetry and stories were often told, rather than written down, and passed through generations from one person to the next. Poems could be about anything to do with everyday life, like going fishing. But sometimes they were about religion, and sometimes were spoken for the gods.

Aztec language was called Nahuatl. All Aztec children went to school, and it was believed that education made a person better. Everyone could take part in storytelling and poetry.

Cortés was a Spanish conqueror who arrived in Mesoamerica looking for land to conquer and opportunities to make money. Cortés and his men landed at Cozumel in 1519.

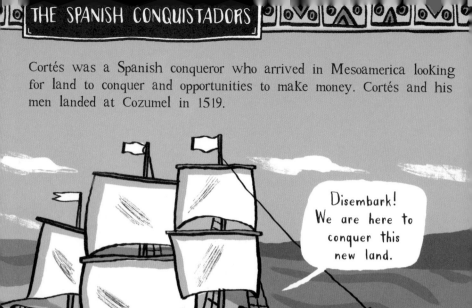

Soon after they arrived, they began to hear stories of a great and rich kingdom inland. Cortés became obsessed with this distant place that the local leaders kept pointing toward. He was looking for what was known as "the great city of Mexico."

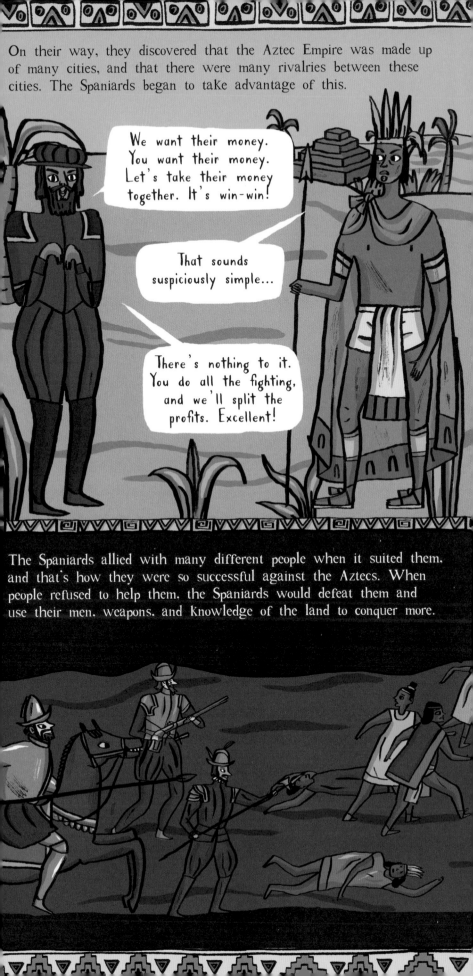

On their way, they discovered that the Aztec Empire was made up of many cities, and that there were many rivalries between these cities. The Spaniards began to take advantage of this.

We want their money. You want their money. Let's take their money together. It's win-win!

That sounds suspiciously simple...

There's nothing to it. You do all the fighting, and we'll split the profits. Excellent!

The Spaniards allied with many different people when it suited them, and that's how they were so successful against the Aztecs. When people refused to help them, the Spaniards would defeat them and use their men, weapons, and knowledge of the land to conquer more.

CORTÉS AND MOCTEZUMA II

Moctezuma II was the ruler of the Aztecs when Cortés invaded Tenochtitlán. When they arrived, Moctezuma welcomed them into his lavish palace and gave them silver and gold, believing Cortés could be the god Quetzalcoatl. But Cortés took Moctezuma hostage.

Both the Spaniards and the Aztecs were suspicious, and the Spaniards started fearing an attack from the Aztecs. So, during a feast in the Great Temple, they ordered the murder of many Aztec nobles and priests. Around the same time, Moctezuma was killed by his own Aztec people for "allying" with the Spaniards. Soon realizing they were outnumbered and surrounded, the Spaniards tried to sneak away...

The Spaniards fought their way out of the city, and many people died. It was Known as the Night of Sadness.

In the next five months, diseases that the Spaniards had brought with them swept through the Aztec Empire. Epidemics of smallpox and the common cold Killed over a third of the population of Mesoamerica.

Then came a final three-month siege on Tenochtitlán. The Spaniards cut off all food and water to the city. The Aztecs were slaughtered and finally succumbed on August 13, 1521. The final Aztec ruler, Cuauhtémoc, was tortured and Killed by Cortés, and the Aztec Empire came to an end.

Do you admit defeat?

Yes. We surrender!

The Aztecs created documents about their society called codices. These are sort of like books, except they're largely created from pictures. They also didn't look like books, as they folded out in an elaborate concertina shape, like this:

But when the Spaniards invaded the Aztec Empire, they saw that codices were part of the Aztec's culture and decided they were dangerous. They wanted to convert them to be Christians like them, and thought taking away their language and culture would help to do this. They destroyed many Aztec codices, though some have survived.

There are also Spanish sources about the Aztec Empire, such as a letter from Cortés to the King of Spain, describing Tenochtitlán.

Historians use such sources to understand Aztec society. But many were written once the Spaniards had arrived, so it can be hard to know what life was really like before that time.

Luckily, archaeologists like me are on hand to help, too!

The Aztecs built amazing buildings and created many beautiful things that have survived down the centuries for us to discover again today. These help us to understand more about Aztec society.

The city of Tenochtitlán, including the Great Temple, is buried under modern Mexico City.

When archaeologists dug up the Great Temple, they found an entire religious quarter. They discovered that the temple had been rebuilt six times in all. The seventh version had been destroyed by the Spaniards in 1521 and the remains were slowly lost under the new city.

Cool, right? Imagine what could be hidden under your city, without you even knowing!

Archaeologists found carvings of animals, statues, beads, and the bones of snakes and birds—which were offerings left by Aztec people for the gods. Objects like shark teeth, tortoise shells, and items made from jade and obsidian tell us more about how materials were traded across the Aztec Empire.

Here are masks made from precious stones like turquoise.

Together, the discoveries of archaeologists and historians help us to know more about how the Aztecs lived.

Isabel Greenberg is a London-based comic
artist, illustrator and writer. She enjoys
illustrating all things historical.

Imogen Greenberg is a London-based writer,
who loves writing about history.

Quarto is the authority on a wide range of topics.

Quarto educates, entertains and enriches the lives of
our readers—enthusiasts and lovers of hands-on living.

www.quartoknows.com

Discover...The Aztec Empire copyright © Frances Lincoln Ltd 2017
Text copyright © Imogen Greenberg 2017
Illustrations copyright © Isabel Greenberg 2017

First published in the USA in 2017 by
Frances Lincoln Children's Books, an imprint of Quarto Inc.,
142 W 36th St, 4th Floor, New York, NY 10018, USA
QuartoKnows.com
Visit our blogs at QuartoKnows.com

ISBN 978-1-84780-950-6
Illustrated digitally

Set in Tom's New Roman and Campland

Printed in China

9 8 7 6 5 4 3 2 1

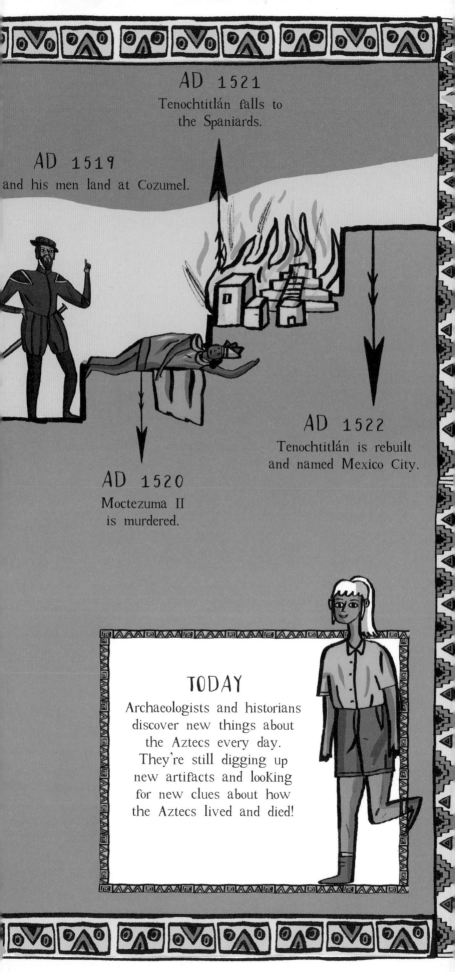

AD 1519

and his men land at Cozumel.

AD 1521

Tenochtitlán falls to
the Spaniards.

AD 1522

Tenochtitlán is rebuilt
and named Mexico City.

AD 1520

Moctezuma II
is murdered.

TODAY

Archaeologists and historians
discover new things about
the Aztecs every day.
They're still digging up
new artifacts and looking
for new clues about how
the Aztecs lived and died!

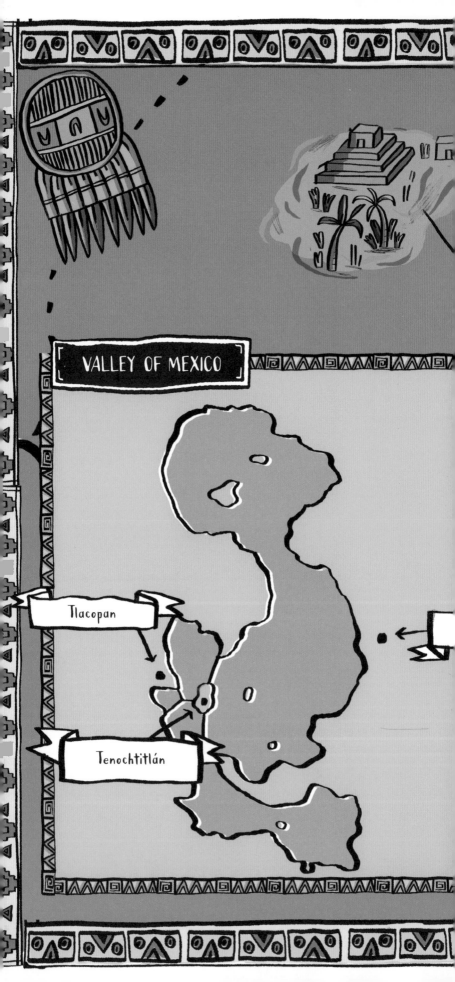

VALLEY OF MEXICO

Tlacopan

Tenochtitlán

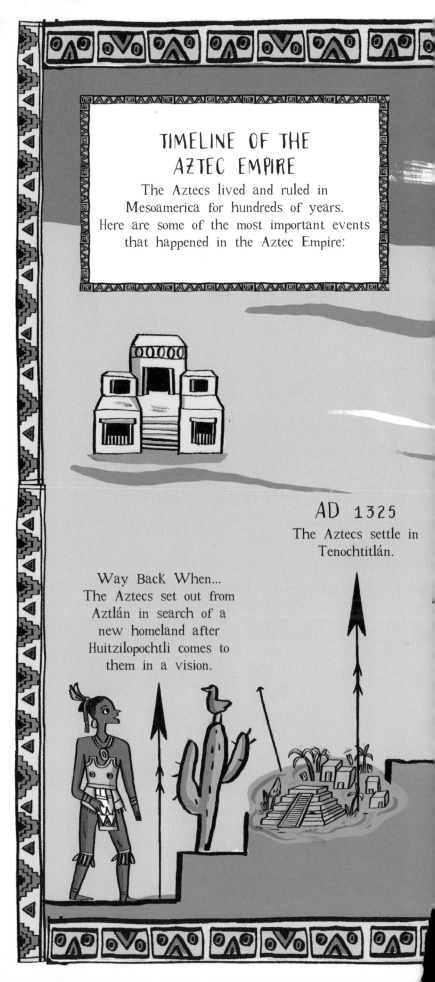

TIMELINE OF THE AZTEC EMPIRE

The Aztecs lived and ruled in Mesoamerica for hundreds of years. Here are some of the most important events that happened in the Aztec Empire:

AD 1325

The Aztecs settle in Tenochtitlán.

Way Back When...
The Aztecs set out from Aztlán in search of a new homeland after Huitzilopochtli comes to them in a vision.

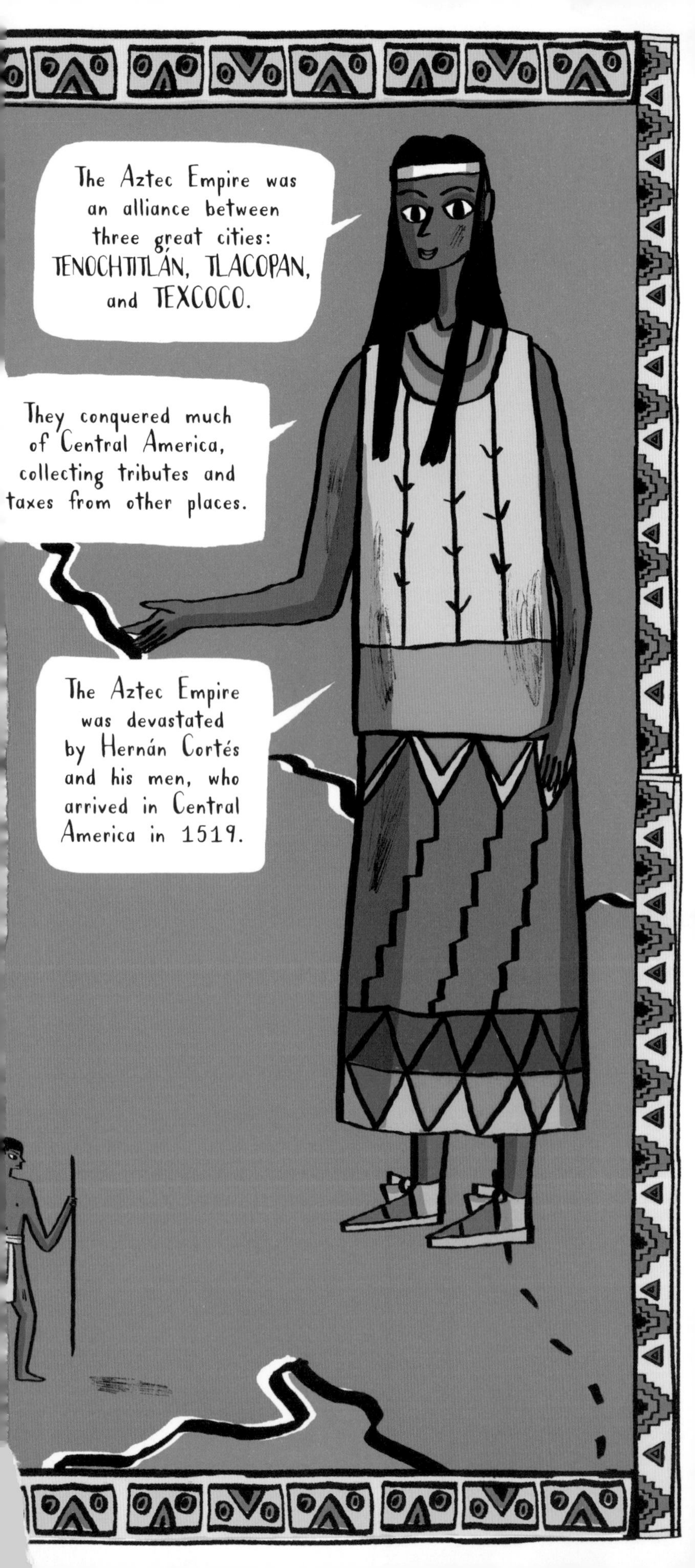
The Aztec Empire was an alliance between three great cities: TENOCHTITLÁN, TLACOPAN, and TEXCOCO.
They conquered much of Central America, collecting tributes and taxes from other places.
The Aztec Empire was devastated by Hernán Cortés and his men, who arrived in Central America in 1519.

THE AZTEC EMPIRE

Texcoco

Cortés

AD 1428/31
The Aztecs join forces with the rulers of Texcoco and Tlacopan to form the Triple Alliance.

AD 1390
The Aztecs begin building the Great Temple.

AD 1502
Moctezuma II becomes ruler o the Aztecs.

AD 1396
Huitzilihuitl becomes ruler of the Aztecs.

AD 1376
Acamapichtli becomes the first Aztec ruler.

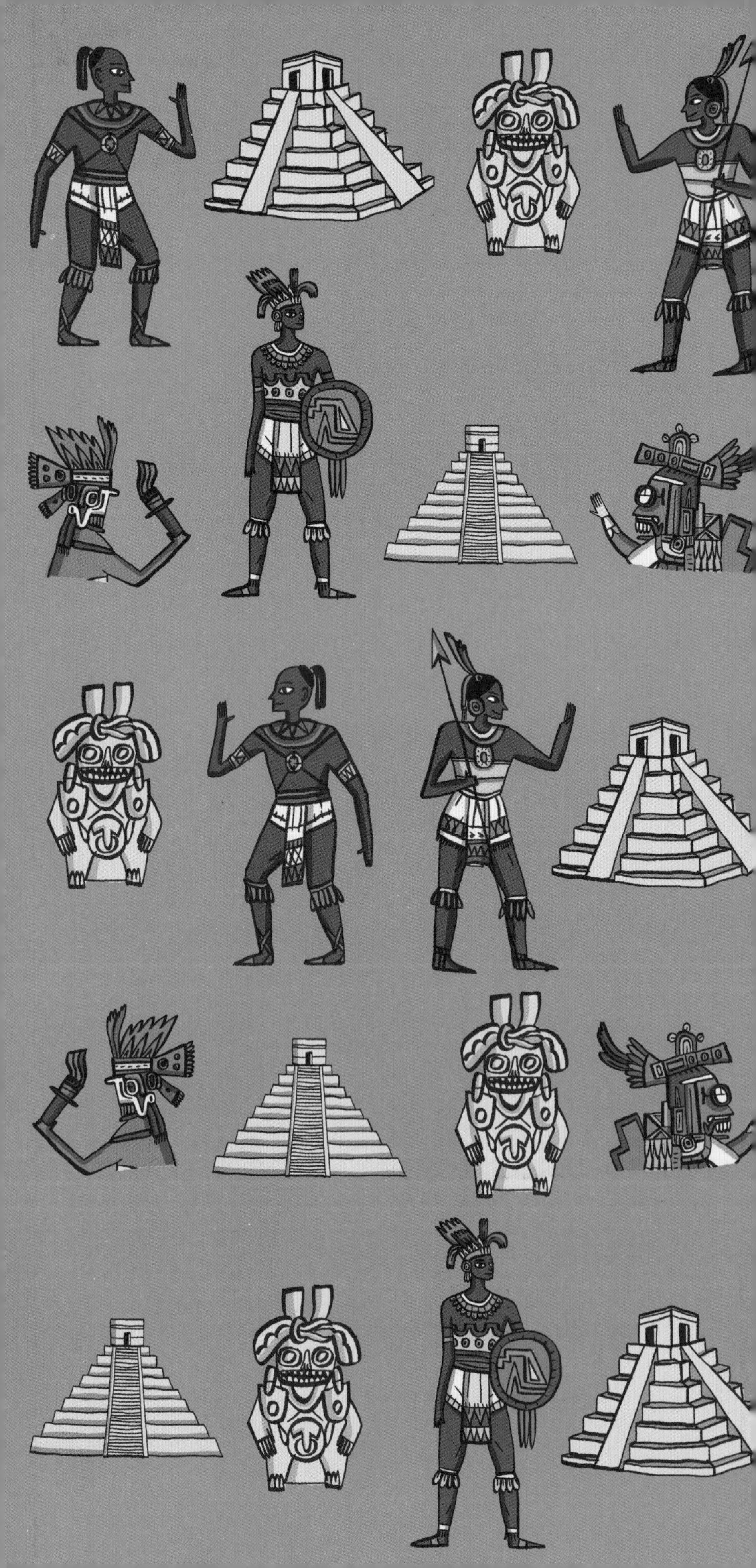